Given to me by
Gary Dulabaum.
We stopped at the
Boardwalk in Laramie.
where he bought AnnMarie
a present. We explored
the area around John
while I read some
of these poems.

DREAMWEAVING
A Journal for Dreamers

BY MARY SOJOURNER

NORTHLAND PUBLISHING

For you, weaver, for solitude and love,

for Light and joy in life,

that you may spin all you want and need.

Copyright © 1991 BY NORTHLAND PUBLISHING CO., INC.

ALL RIGHTS RESERVED

This book may not be reproduced in whole or in part
by any means without permission of the publisher.
For information address Northland Publishing Co.,
P.O. Box 1389, Flagstaff, AZ 86002.

FIRST EDITION
SECOND PRINTING, 1993

ISBN 0-87358-516-X

LIBRARY OF CONGRESS CATALOG CARD NUMBER 90-53594

Designed by Carolyn Gibbs
Jacket design by David Jenney

MANUFACTURED IN THE UNITED STATES OF AMERICA
BY HART GRAPHICS

Where you are, believe it or not, is at the very center of life.

It is precious beyond your recognition. Cherish it.

Be more careful than you have these past days. Really.

April Delaney, in
THE MAGIC JOURNEY
by John Nichols

IN SISTERS OF THE DREAM, LIZ MORRIGAN MOVES TO A
MOUNTAIN TOWN IN ARIZONA AND DREAMS THE LIFE OF
TALASI, A TWELFTH-CENTURY HOPI WOMAN. DREAMS GUIDED
MY STORY OF THEIR STORIES. DREAMS GUIDED ME TO THIS
WORK. DREAMS BRING SISTERS TOGETHER. WE INVITE YOU TO
JOIN US.

—·—

AT WINTER SOLSTICE, the oldest woman speaks:
"How good it is to be in this circle, my kin, and
to see your faces, you women, you men, you
children and old ones. You are all colors and you are beautiful; your eyes of sky, of water, of earth, all shining in the
firelight that illuminates this longest night, this brief
story, this dream.

"My name is Cerridwen, or perhaps Hecate, or Acca; or
is it Tlatentli or Tiamat or Kohkyangwuhti? I am very old.
Time blurs, and names. You have given me so many, as you
have named the stars, the flowers, the birds and snakes and
mountains. I am Dreamweaver. As are you."

from SISTERS OF THE DREAM

Imagine this, my kin,

that dreams are only

pathways through time

and trails through

possibility.

Tonight, or on

a lazy afternoon,

lie down before

you are really tired.

Be comfortable.

Feel your breath.

Know it is the Dreampath.

Imagine that some

may be strong enough

to travel these pathways...

where would you travel?

...In this dream,

in this bright darkness,

I travel long ago

and far ahead.

In this circle,

in this story,

listening and dreaming,

you may travel with me.

We begin.

As in any journey,

travelling the Dreampath

is more delightful when

you take a few treasures

with you. You might place

around your pillow,

over your heart, on a shelf

or window sill near your bed,

a feather, a stone, a picture

of a beloved place or person(s)...

All dreams spin out

from the same web.

As the fire cast its shadows

on the stone walls,

she dozed, grateful to be

in the dreaming world.

It seemed to her

that her dead grandmother,

Sihu, spoke with her

from the other side.

It was beautiful there,

all cool greenish mist,

the color of the sohovi *leaves.*

You might envision

your Dreampath,

your dreaming world.

Slow your breathing,

let your breath move

out from you, into dark,

into light, into mist

or bright sunlight...

...AND YOUR DREAM HELPERS,

YOUR SWEET, COURAGEOUS GUIDES

AND COMPANIONS...CHOOSE THEM

CAREFULLY!

*Star shadows played
against the raw wood walls.
The big pines creaked
in the wind. By Liz's side,
the new cat, the silver gray,
settled in to nurse
its tail and purr.*

THE WAKING WORLD, THE RAIN

ON YOUR WINDOW, THE MUSIC

MOVING IN THE AIR, THE FIRE,

IF YOU ARE LUCKY, CRACKLING

IN THE WOODSTOVE, THE JUNIPER

SMOKE YOU HAVE TRAILED

ROUND YOUR BED, FOR BLESSING

AND PROTECTION...THEY CAN SLIP

THROUGH THE DREAMVEIL,

INTO YOUR DREAMS...

Talasi, drifting in and out

of dreams, heard the rasp

of her mother's work,

the music of the grinding,

the music of her mother's songs

and saw, behind her closed owl

eyes, the Spirits dancing high

above, laughing and playing,

bounding from star to star.

Prepare for dreams

as you would prepare

for a lover. Cradle

your body and spirit

as you would a child.

She settled herself and Talasi

into a pile of robes

and began to sing.

It was a song to Father Sun,

a song to Mother Earth,

to She who gave

and received all beings,

all juniper and corn and pine,

all eagles and snakes,

all children, all Old Ones,

all life...

ALL DREAMS ARE GIFTS,

ALL ARE LESSONS;

ALL ARE INVITATIONS

TO THE SACRED DANCE...

THAT IS OUR LIFE.

THERE ARE NO NIGHTMARES...

THOSE POWERFUL DREAMS

ARE SHE-HORSES, EAGER MOUNTS

FOR WANDERERS, GREAT, DELICATE

ANIMALS SNIFFING THE AIR,

SURE-FOOTED ON UNKNOWN TRAILS.

By daylight,

the great desert spaces

had been unsettling,

but in starlight,

with the glowing hills

coiled around,

Liz felt quite safe.

She understood how

a woman or man

might simply start walking

and never stop.

Our wishes are our dreams,

our dreams, our wishes...

...Liz wanted to stand in the sun

and shadow of those ruined walls.

She wanted to enter the doorways.

She wanted to set her hands

on that warm stone.

Doorways. Windows. Arches.

A dream might be a gift

wrapped in black paper,

splashed with silver Orion

and the shining Pleiades.

How the moon invites us in.

How the sun warms our closed

eyelids. Dreams. And, for you,

how do they beckon?

The lake was a sheet

of black glass. The moon

was mirrored there, cool, full,

working its power where it could,

on the tides of heart and brain;

and to the west, washing over

that warm rock.

If we wore our dreams

around our necks,

they would form

a chain of light.

Hanging from each link

would be a stone of power...

garnet for heart, turquoise

for joy, opal for sight...

and your stones, name them,

want them, receive them

as they come to you.

Find your "something beautiful."

Braid silk or cotton or leather

or yucca or red cedar bark.

Suspend your dream talisman

from it. Every time you touch

or see it, wish yourself dreams.

Alone Liz felt invisible.

Alone she was most ordinary,

alone, no miracle at all.

You dream alone.
Visible. Invisible,
moving into
a delicate world..
journeying alone.

ALONE, YOU ARE...

DREAMING, YOU ARE...

Sleep was holding out

for something special.

Liz tensed her body

and let it go....

She counted breaths.

She thought of old riddles

and made up new ones.

Sleep holds out for something
special. So do dreams.
Ask your dreams to tell you
how to sleep. Listen for
the answers. Watch.

An old woman leads you

on a path. Perhaps you need

to walk. *There is a banquet.*

You are the guest.

Perhaps it is time

to nourish yourself...

Behind her closed lids,

Liz fixed that perfect circle,

that shimmer, absolute white

against absolute black.

She breathed into it,

submerged, felt herself soar out,

slip away, let go, come back,

again and again, to that circle

of light, that circle...

CLOSE YOUR EYES. BREATHE DEEP.

BREATHE GENTLY. DRIFT BACK

THROUGH YOUR DAY.

WHAT PICTURE COMES TO MIND?

SUNRISE, A FACE, BLOSSOM,

YOUR CAT LOOKING UP AT YOU

AS THOUGH YOU WERE DAFT;

AN ONION SLICE, PURPLE

AND TRANSLUCENT, FALLING

PERFECT AWAY FROM YOUR KNIFE;

THE MOON...

You might create your dream mandala here. If you think you must be an artistic genius, must make the perfect picture, find a fat crayon and scribble a great mess on this page...

Having not remembered

a dream for days, I drift

into sleep. *A great white bird*

flies straight toward my face.

I wonder if it is a holy ghost.

Her head is made of light.

I wake. I see her in my sleep

for weeks. She becomes that

which I follow to guide myself

into sleep.

The fire cast slivers of orange

on the ceiling, bright against

the trail of cool starlight

from the west window.

Liz let herself float in

and out of that haze

that is not quite sleep;

the dream teased.

ARE THERE CANDLES

AROUND YOUR BED?

DOES MUSIC PLAY SOFTLY

AS YOU FLOAT SOMEWHERE

BETWEEN DREAM AND WAKING,

WAKING AND DREAM?

DID YOU KNOW THAT

IN SOME COUNTRIES

WOMEN WEAVE DREAMCATCHERS

FROM WIRE AND THREAD

AND BEADS? MIGHT YOU?

Liz struggled up

from dreamless sleep.

It was a surfacing

from bad water

with a body

that had forgotten

how to swim

and a spirit

that would have settled

for drowning.

ANY DREAM IS BETTER

THAN NO DREAM.

More women than men
remember their dreams.
If you are a man,
spend a whole day
doing nothing useful
and/or important, and see
what the night brings.
If you are a woman,
be grateful.

Sometimes in the early morning,

on the path, Liz heard the hiss

of traffic on the highway

beyond the trees, but, in the cabin,

there was always a hush.

She dozed, half-hearing

the whisper of the fire,

feeling its perfect warmth

along her side.

WHAT DO YOU HEAR

IN THE HOUR BEFORE YOU SLEEP?

HOW IS IT DREAMCATCHING?

HOW IS IT NOT? WHAT WOULD IT

TAKE TO MAKE IT PERFECT?

WHAT WOULD YOU GIVE?

Liz had once said

to her students,

"If we see ourselves

solely through men's eyes,

then every one of us

in this room

will disappear

before she dies."

IN OUR DREAMS,

WE SEE OURSELVES SOLELY

THROUGH OUR OWN EYES.

SOMETIMES WITHOUT A LENS

BETWEEN SELF AND SEER,

SOMETIMES AS THOUGH

THROUGH A CRYSTAL

OR KALEIDOSCOPE.

Dreams defy

symbolic systems.

They, do, however,

love to dance.

Liz closed her eyes.

The jay went silent.

She could hear

the cats slipping

through the dry grass.

Sun beat on her face,

burning in behind

her bones, her eyelids;

rose-red, steady.

SLEEP OUTDOORS.

BE EIGHT AGAIN.

CAMP IN THE BACKYARD.

SLEEP ON THE ROOF.

MAY YOU LIVE IN A WORLD

SAFE ENOUGH TO DO THAT.

WE CAN DREAM OF THAT

FOR EVERYONE.

IF YOU DREAM THE SAFE-WORLD

DREAM, ASK YOUR DREAMS

TO TELL YOU HOW TO AWAKEN IT.

PAY ATTENTION. DO WHAT YOU'RE

TOLD. ONCE, IN A WAKING DREAM,

MY HANDS FLAT AGAINST

RED EARTH, I ASKED AND

WAS TOLD, *SLOW DOWN*.

Liz jolted awake.

A cold wind had come up.

Clouds dimmed the setting sun.

She felt the dream hover,

as real and elusive

as the scudding clouds.

WHAT DAY DREAMS

DRIFT AND RACE FOR YOU,

AS CLOUD, AS SUN,

AS REAL AS FOG,

AND AS ELUSIVE?

The night was strange, off-key,

in that way of new places,

so that place and memory

interweave imperfectly, and jar.

TAKE YOURSELF SOMEWHERE NEW

TO SLEEP...A BEACH, CREEKSIDE,

BASE OF A GREAT PINE, MOUNTAIN

OR BACK PORCH, MOTEL OR LIVING-

ROOM FLOOR, YOUR CHILD'S BED...

IF YOU SLEEP WITH SOMEONE,

SLEEP ALONE; IF YOU SLEEP ALONE,

SPEND THE NIGHT WITH A FRIEND.

Navajo women weave

a spirit line into their work,

a few plain threads that run

straight from the rug's heart

to its outside edge. It guarantees

that the woman will not become

trapped in her work.

ALL DREAMS ARE SPIRIT LINES.

Talasi tried to raise her head,

but when she looked, the tall

red house on its boulder

doubled and blurred.

"Stop, father," she cried.

"My aunt's house is many

and the great rock is sliding

into the ground." She threw

her arms up over her eyes.

ALL DREAMS ARE SPIRIT LINES...

SHE-HORSES...LESSONS FROM

A FIERCE AND LOVING TEACHER.

Much later,

as the fire went to coals

and the crescent moon

appeared in the skylight,

Liz pulled the quilts

up over her body

and whispered into them,

"I'd like a dream, a gift,

and to remember."

How can we ask

an unknown Dreamweaver

for the gift of our dreams?

To meet your Dreamweaver,

that dear friend, that fierce

and loving teacher,

let yourself imagine,

let yourself see and hear

and touch and smell

and taste your favorite place

in all this universe...

Settle in to that magic place
as it lies deep within you.
Let someone, something be
there with you. Recognize it.
For some, it is an animal,
for others, a person,
for yet others, light or wind
or water. Call it by name.
Dreamweaver. Let it teach you.

Pamosi crouched over Talasi,

bent to the task. She felt,

she saw nothing but the girl.

She was nothing more than clay,

pliable in the Spirit's hands.

The healing moved through her,

cool and strong. What she did

was as wonderful and impossible

as flight.

DREAMS MOVE THROUGH YOU.

IN SLEEP YOU ARE NOTHING

MORE THAN CLAY, PLIABLE...

WHAT DREAMS DO, WHAT YOU DO

IS AS WONDERFUL AND IMPOSSIBLE

AS FLIGHT.

That night, Liz dreamed

of Hatt Latham.

It was a simple dream.

Hatt lay subdued

and silent in her bed.

Liz bent over her,

pleading with her

to get up, to fight,

to talk...

SOME DREAMS WEAVE

IN THE LOOSE THREADS

OF OUR DAY. THEY TEACH US

WHAT OUR NEXT STRONG STEPS

MIGHT BE.

[The dream being]

dripped the sweet rain

from his hands to her lips.

Talasi tasted cornmeal

and red berries

and baked squash

fresh from the fields.

IN YOUR DREAMING

TASTE FULLY WHAT IS GIVEN

TO YOU TO EAT.

IN YOUR WAKING

PAY NO LESS ATTENTION.

[The dream being]

held out to Talasi

a shimmering seed of light;

it trembled and melted

and re-formed, perhaps scarlet,

perhaps purple as the far desert,

perhaps blue, perhaps green

as the new shoots of spring.

Talasi reached out.

Accept all dream-gifts.

In waking, watch for them

to reappear. Their form

may differ, their heart

will be the same. The living

diamonds of the dream-snake

may be painted on a bowl.

The explosion that so

frightened you, a fine,

clean burst of rage....

Talasi laughed..."It is

the guiding stone for my path...

I will carry it with me

for a long time." She closed

her fingers. When she opened

them, the stone was gone.

"This is her mystery,"

Toho said..."It is her secret."

YOUR DREAMS ARE YOURS...

TO WRITE, TO PAINT, TO TELL,

TO HOLD SECRET IN THE SAFE

PLACES OF YOUR HEART.

That night, sleep

moved into Liz easily,

as though earned,

as natural as breath,

as welcome as a dear,

familiar lover.

FOR SOME OF US, SLEEP IS A LOVER,

FOR SOME A GREAT UNKNOWN,

FOR OTHERS A REMINDER

OF SAFE TIMES, AND FOR MANY,

THE CLOSED DOOR TO CHILDHOOD

TERRORS AND HORRORS

WE MIGHT SOMEDAY UNCOVER.

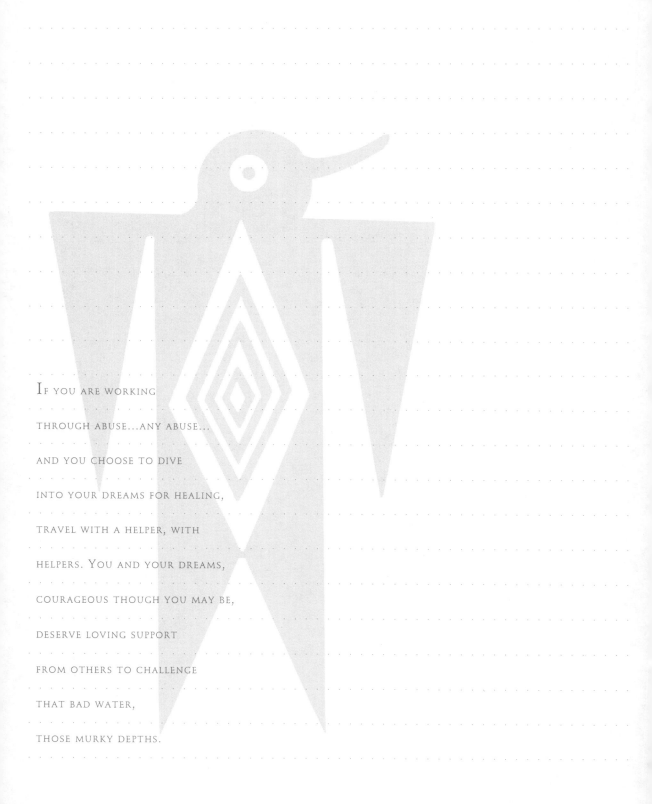

If you are working

through abuse...any abuse...

and you choose to dive

into your dreams for healing,

travel with a helper, with

helpers. You and your dreams,

courageous though you may be,

deserve loving support

from others to challenge

that bad water,

those murky depths.

Talasi lay awake.

She could hear

her mother and father

talking softly. Most nights,

the gentle rise

and fall of their voices

was a song to sleep by.

She could ride

on the gentle waves,

letting herself slip

deeper and deeper

into her dreaming.

But, this night,

there were long silences...

Your childhood bed,
the sounds and silence
in that place.
What do you remember?
Do you remember?

AND THAT DREAM

THAT RECURRED AND RECURRED,

PERHAPS A BELOVED VISITOR,

PERHAPS A BAD GUEST,

WHAT DO YOU REMEMBER?

HOW DO YOU SEE IT NOW?

WHAT WAS IT TELLING YOU?

Liz shivered. The raven

had flown northeast.

That seemed a good direction,

but she did not know why.

Something about the dream

lay that way.

If a bird carried you

into your dreams,

what bird would it be?

Raven? Jay? Hummingbird?

Hawk or sparrow or kite?

How are you like

that dream-bird?

Give yourself this gift:

in some dream in the future,

perhaps this afternoon

or tonight or tomorrow

morning, perhaps a year

from now, or seven, let

yourself know you are

dreaming. Look around.

Learn in which direction

your dream moves. In which

direction you move.

"Lady," he said, "I'd have
to be a dreamer to do this,
chasing down radioactive
tailings, reminding nice people
day after day not to pick up
arrow points and bones
and nine-hundred-year-old
pottery pieces and put them in
their hundred-dollar backpacks..."

Some dreams remind us to *be* dreamers, to remember that we are children of this Earth, and She is longing for our dreams and caring. She dreams us as we dream Her; we must care for Her as She cares for us.

The mesa was blurred...
as though Liz looked
through a pane of ice.
She remembered playing
near a creek, in December
twilight, lifting a sheet
of ice from the black water
to her eye and seeing dried
grasses like plumes of light...

If we ignore our dreams,

they may occupy our waking,

sliding into place before us

as a lens, through which we see

that which must be known,

that which must be discovered,

that which must be lived

and done.

Liz finished the water

and turned on her side.

There was snowlight

through the crystal tumbler,

blue-white, splintered, fragile...

For writers: I LIVED THIS

BEFORE I DREAMED IT, DREAMED IT

BEFORE I WROTE IT, HAVE WRITTEN

CROSSROADS ON MY PATH

BEFORE I CAME TO THEM.

FOR THOSE WHO BELIEVE

THEY CANNOT WRITE: YOU CAN.

...the children, the path,

the violet shadows were gone

and Liz stood in blackness.

There was no sound.

There was nothing

but her breath, her heartbeat

and the cold floor

under her bare feet.

She knew she was dreaming.

She knew it would be

easy to wake.

In your dreams,

you may come to

this place of no-place.

When you do,

you will be ready

to rest there,

you will be ready

to hear what the dark,

the cold, the silence

have to teach you.

"I will stay this time," Liz said.

"Not yet," the being said,

and laughed softly. "You have

always been in such a hurry."

Imagine you could guide

yourself through your

dreams; know that might be

only an imagining.

"I can't remember the other dreams," Liz said, "just this one."

"Write it down," Deena said.

"You're supposed to be the expert."

You ARE the expert.

Write down your dream

from the viewpoint

of anyone, anything but you.

Be the car, your mother,

the sparrow, the saguaro,

the house over your head,

the road under your feet.

Do it with everything,

everybody in the dream.

Ask those experts!

Liz opened the desk drawer

and took out the journal.

She had no plantings,

no births or deaths,

no illnesses; not one recipe,

and there was no medicine

for what ailed her.

DREAMS AND YOUR JOURNAL
ARE OLD MEDICINE. YOUR WORDS
MIGHT BE JUNIPER, LAVENDER
OR TANSY; SAGE OR OSHA, YERBA
SANTE OR JOHN THE CONGEROO
ROOT. THESE PAGES ARE PARCHMENT,
PAPYRUS, ARE SAND ON WHICH
AN OLD, OLD WOMAN SCRATCHES
THE VEGETABLE SECRETS FOR LIFE
AND DEATH.

Liz scattered dry sage

on the woodstove top

and breathed deep.

It smelled like summer

on the South Rim

of the Canyon. She thought

of that great stony light

and of the tourists,

how some were struck silent

as they came upon it.

BURN SAGE, BURN SWEET GRASS,

COPAL OR AMBER. STROKE A FEW

DROPS OF PERFUME OR HERBAL OIL

ON YOUR PILLOW, ON YOUR THROAT

AND WRISTS. LET YOUR DREAMS

MOVE WHERE THE SCENT TAKES YOU.

In any season,

open your window

and let the night air

fill the room.

Soar on it.

Dive into it.

If you are tempted

to learn another's symbols

for *your* dreams,

let that teaching

rest lightly in your heart.

A tree is a tower is a man

is a woman is a way

to break up the light,

to reflect it, to eat it

and let it shine.

LET SYMBOLS REST LIGHTLY

IN YOUR HEART. LET GUIDANCE

LEAVE ROOM FOR DREAMS.

Talasi trembled

under her robes,

shuddering into dreams,

waking again and again,

her heart cold as stone

in her breast...

Talasi woke.

The room was black.

She heard her mother

turn in her sleep,

her father cough.

She wanted to wake them,

to tell them the dream,

but sleep silenced her...

Our dreams are friends
that teach friendship.
Do you have someone
you can call on
those stone-cold nights?
If not, ask your dreams
to show you the path
to that friend.

On the trail of a dream-friend,

on those stone-cold nights,

keep this journal by your bed.

Move out of sleep's silence

and write. As you would turn

to a friend, as you would turn

to yourself.

Around Talasi's neck

hung a string of young

antelope backbones

and from each bone

hung a hawk feather,

pale gray, striped

and tipped with brown.

She felt very light,

as though her flesh

was woven on twisted fiber,

as though she were no more

than a robe.

As you drift into sleep tonight, picture your warrior's necklace; see the feathers, feel the weight of the bones or beads or stones. Sleep. Watch where the necklace carries you.

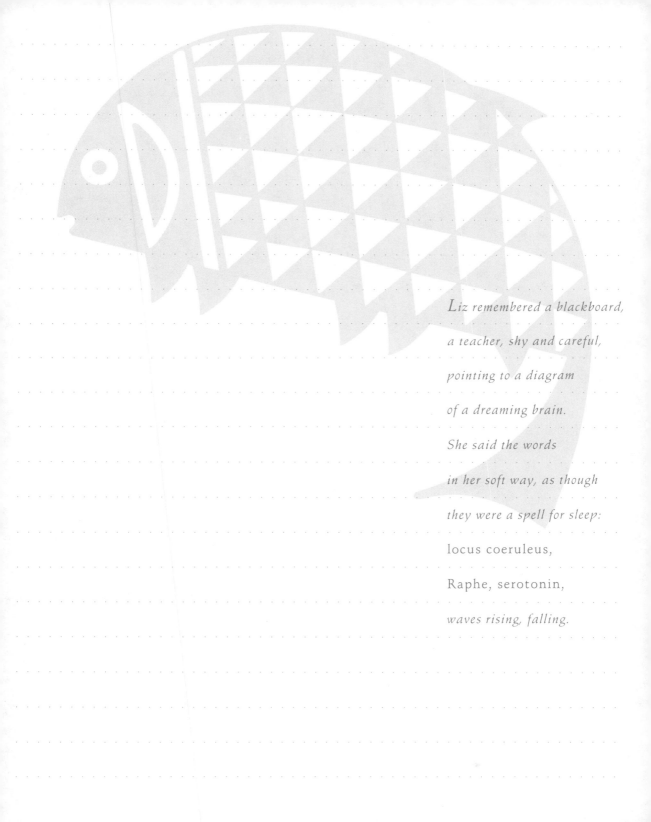

Liz remembered a blackboard,

a teacher, shy and careful,

pointing to a diagram

of a dreaming brain.

She said the words

in her soft way, as though

they were a spell for sleep:

locus coeruleus,

Raphe, serotonin,

waves rising, falling.

Take away dream time

and the brain was in agony.

Hallucinations shimmered

in full daylight. Voices carried

messages from nowhere.

And in the outback,

in the Dream Time,

the messages shimmered

and echoed, the dreams dying,

the brain a howl...

When your brain howls,
when your body burns
and aches, when you believe
you have been abandoned,
or you feel someone,
something closing you in
so you cannot breathe,
take a day. Do nothing.
Sleep when you are tired.
Eat when you are hungry.
Move when you must. Dream.

Know that alcohol,

marijuana, coffee, sugar,

amphetamines, tranquilizers,

bad love, bad work,

too little sleep,

too much food

stun the Dreamweaver,

put that Great Helper

to work defending

your dreams, leave It

little time to weave

the stories that help you

make it through the night.

Kihsi, the shadow

that moves as light,

in silence, slipped through

the village, never taking

his eyes from the girl perched

above him on the rooftop.

He settled into a narrow alley

and watched Second Dawn

shine off her hair.

Good love, good work,

how they shine in us,

how our dreams tell clues

to what they might be,

how we might bring them

dawning into our waking lives.

FRIENDSHIP IS THE DAWN
OF GOOD LOVE AND THE HIGH NOON
AND THE LAST, SWEET OPAL LIGHT
OF EVENING. DREAM OF THAT.
LET YOURSELF WAKE TO IT.

"I'll tell you the dream," Liz said.

"All you have to do is listen."

Deena sat up on the countertop.

"I'm ready," she said.

On this page, if you wish, write a letter to the friend who is ready, the friend who sits and listens, the friend you are lucky enough to have, or wise enough to seek. Tell your friend a dream that haunts you.

"There were circles everywhere,"

Liz said. "The plaza, a playing

field, the way some boulders

were set in the sand."

    "Oh, wow," Deena said.

    "I know," Liz laughed.

"Sym-bolic!"

The dream that haunts you,

the blue-black clouds,

the huge, faceless thing

that chases you down alleys

to a cliff and no way out

but leaping. Feel yourself

on the other side of the clouds,

in rose-gold light, feel yourself

turn and face the faceless

thing and watch it change,

feel yourself step off the cliff...

Talasi swallowed

the questions that were

in her throat.

She felt them settle

in her heart.

They rested there,

as her breath slowed

under Pamosi's touch

and she moved into sleep.

In your dream,

this one or the next,

feel who you touch,

who touches you.

If there is no one,

move out in your

waking to touching.

If you are engulfed

with dream-touch,

move out in your

waking to solitude,

to only the wind

or light on your skin.

Spend a day doing nothing,

sleeping when you're tired,

eating when you're hungry,

moving when you must,

listening to nothing

but wind and heartbeat.

Follow the fullness

of that into the hollow

bowl of your dream.

IN A TIME

OF DREAMLESSNESS,

LISTEN TO OTHERS.

WE ARE SHY

ABOUT OUR WAKING.

BUT A CHILD,

AN OLD ONE,

A STRANGER,

NOT YET KNOWN...

THEY WILL TELL

THEIR DREAMS.

AND YOU

MIGHT LISTEN.

Liz opened the vents.

Wet pine air poured in.

Orion floated frozen

just above the horizon....

She thought of sleep,

peaceful, and how it

had become a door

and she drove toward it...

THROUGH THE DOOR OF SLEEP,

INTO THE CORRIDORS OF DREAMS,

HAVING BROUGHT YOURSELF

TO THIS HOME, YOU MIGHT FIND

YOURSELF DREAMING AND KNOW

YOU DREAM. YOU SEE BEFORE YOU

AN ENDLESS LINE OF LOCKLESS

DOORS. YOU PAUSE.

IMAGINE THAT INSTANT

WHEN YOU KNOW

YOU ARE IN A DREAM,

YOU KNOW YOU CAN

GO ANYWHERE.

YOU CAN ASK A QUESTION.

YOU CAN FOLLOW

THE SHINING THREAD

THAT LEADS YOU

TO THE BEGINNINGS

OF THE ANSWER.

Once, when I was thirty-seven and more frightened that I had ever imagined possible, I felt my breath stop in my body. It happened again and again. I knew what it was to follow my breath and that path was agony.

That night, for the first time,

I "woke" in my dream. I knew

I was dreaming. I remembered

I could ask a question:

What must I do to breathe¿

Stairs opened up in front

of me and led to a book

on an old, walnut podium.

The book lay open to a sky-

chart. The stars began

to dance. I watched and saw

the page turn. Glittering silver

letters formed on the dark

paper: *Make love with yourself.*

I woke to the dawn
and listened to the whisper
of the boughs. The birds
began to chitter. The old,
black cat settled in at my side.
I lay still and saw and heard
and, miracle, felt my breath
whispering in and out
of my breast.

Liz shivered.

The door of sleep

lay half-open.

She turned

from the day

that lay ahead

and went through...

Morning. You wake with the question in your heart. Work pulls you forward, the day marked off into neat and hungry segments. They will eat your time. You close your eyes. You pull the door wide open.

Liz went to sleep

early that night...

she had hiked half the day

in a little side canyon,

found a tiny purple shell

on a cliff-ledge.

It was a perfect mystery.

PERFECT MYSTERIES:

HOW THE RED-TAIL HAWK

FEATHER DRIFTED DOWN

WHERE I WAS WALKING,

HOW YOU ANSWERED MY CALL,

HOW I CALLED.

PERFECT MYSTERY #1: HOW

WE DRIFT, HOW WE LEAVE, HOW

WE STAY, HOW WE KNOW WHAT

MYSTERIES SUSTAIN US, WHAT

ORDINARY MIRACLES LEAP UP

FROM OUR HEARTS, INTO OUR

DREAMS, INTO OUR WAKING.

Driving back

to Deena's car,

they were both quiet.

Home, Liz made a fire

and that, too, was fine,

to feel tired and peaceful,

to see the light dancing

like Northern Lights

on the dark ceiling.

PERFECT MYSTERY #2: HOW

EVERY MOMENT IS A DREAM,

AND WE ARE AS FREE TO ASK

OUR QUESTIONS AND RECEIVE

OUR ANSWERS, AS THOUGH

IN DREAMS, AS THOUGH

IN PERFECT SAFETY.

Liz tapped the rattle

against her hand

and closed her eyes...

it gave sea-waves on sand,

sleet on windowpanes,

a diamondback's warning,

a mother's hush to calm

a frightened child.

We know how to call

in waking dreams.

A rattle, a drum, music,

our body moving

through the spiral dance

that takes us home,

that takes us dreaming.

Into the heart of the matter.

Into the heart of the mystery.

Here are some Dreamweavers ,

who snare me and set me free:

Lisa Thiel, Brooke Medicine

Eagle, the Shartse Tibetan

Buddhist monks, Walt

Richardson and the Morning

Star band, The Who, Clapton,

Tina Turner and Koko Taylor.

Behind her closed eyes,

against that green light,

Liz saw people dancing,

and corn tassels, and flat figures

with great eyes, their mouths

unmoving and silent. She

saw something golden struggling

in light and shadow. Human

or other...she could not tell.

REMEMBER, THAT WHICH VISITS

FROM YOUR DREAMING IS WISE.

REMEMBER, THE LENS WE BRING

TO THE VISION IS OURS.

"But, without you,"

Liz said, "I've come here.

And there's peace here.

And dreams."

WITHIN YOU, WITHIN ME,

WITHOUT HER OR HIM

OR GIN OR TOBACCO

OR TOO MUCH FOOD

OR TOO LITTLE,

OR WORK AND NO PLAY,

WITHOUT THAT WHICH

IS OUR SAFE, SAD SHIELD...

WHAT DREAMS EMERGE,

WHAT TERROR LEAPS OUT,

WHAT JOY.

ONE DREAM

AT A TIME...

YOU KNOW THAT.

WE DREAM AND,

IN THE DREAMING,

ONLY DREAM.

"What?"

Talasi whispered.

The air shimmered

to her heart-side.

Light flickered

across the path.

She bowed her head.

"As You wish,"

she whispered.

As you wish, dreamer.

Meet who and what you wish,
visitors and visions from
this time and from times
far past. For some of us,
the future leans in
and beckons. As you wish.

The light stopped,

drew in on itself,

burning brighter

and brighter

till she could not look.

When Talasi

raised her eyes,

she saw the woman,

a woman who raised

her eyes to Talasi...

In perfect Hopilavayi,

Talasi heard the woman's words:

"I am Elizabeth Margaret,"

she said, "and you are Talasi.

I have been dreaming of you."

And I, of you, Talasi thought

and smiled to see the woman nod...

SOMETIMES IN DREAMS

MY FRIEND MICHAEL,

DEAD SINCE 1978, VISITS.

I AM HAPPY TO SEE HIM.

I AM NOT SURPRISED.

"Hey," Liz said, "I'm okay."

"Good," Deena said.

"I had no doubts."

"Thank you."

"Sweet dreams."

THIS DREAMWEAVING IS ENDING.

SWEETLY. LET IT FALL BEHIND YOU,

AS A TRAIL MIGHT, A TRAIL THAT

CAN BE TRAVELLED AGAIN AND AGAIN,

A LITTLE OR A LOT DIFFERENT,

NEVER THE SAME, YIELDING UP

OLD TREASURES, SURPRISING YOU

WITH NEW DELIGHTS.